The Silent

Written by Glynne MacLean

Illustrated by Steve Dininno

Procession

"Who are they?" asked Gryph, nodding at a small procession of people—teens, adults, and seniors— slow marching, two abreast, down the bus lane. Their smooth, synchronized gait and fixed stares gave them a weird, android-like air.

"Protesters probably," replied Aneesa, peering into her shopping bag.

"They've got no banners, and no one's talking. They're silent."

"Where are we supposed to meet your brother again?" asked Aneesa.

"At the car. Jake's parked at Civic Square," answered Gryph, her eyes on the silent procession. "Ask them what they're marching for."

"You."

"No, you," said Gryph. "If it's against global warming or profiteering oil companies, we could join in." She nudged Aneesa. "You're the greenie. Go on— it might be fun."

"Excuse me," said Aneesa to a bony woman in muddy work boots. "Are you protesters?"

The woman ignored her.

"Try another," said Gryph. "He's cute. You could ask him."

Close Reading

Explain how the author's word choice helps paint a picture of what is happening in the procession.

Aneesa made a face. "I'm not into muscle-bound. I'll ask her." She stepped forward, reaching out to touch a woman in a chef's hat and apron. "Excuse me . . . "

As she made contact, Aneesa's chin snapped up, and her eyes flicked forward. Dropping her shopping bag, she slipped into the procession next to the chef. The person she'd displaced moved a rank back, generating a ripple down the length of the procession.

"Aneesa," bellowed Gryph. "What are you doing?"

She was about to grab Aneesa's arm when she saw the ranks ripple again when another fell into line, just as Aneesa had. Gryph gulped and picked up the discarded shopping bag. Her stomach heaved—this had to be bad.

As Gryph kept pace with the marchers, yelling at Aneesa, the ranks rippled a further three times with new entrants. Through it all, Aneesa remained oblivious, her eyes anchored straight ahead. Gryph paused to text her friends for help before she tried catching up again. As they turned the corner onto High Street, Gryph spotted her older brother Jake, so she jumped and waved until he came to meet her.

"What's the matter with you?" asked Jake.

"It's Aneesa. She's gone android, and it's all my fault. It happens to anyone who touches them. I've seen it. She even dropped her new shoes. She's saved up money for them for months, and she just dropped them. It's horrible, and the line's getting longer—"

"Hey, stop the babbling. Calm down!"

RIGHT BEFORE THEIR EYES, PEOPLE WERE DISAPPEARING INTO THIN AIR

Gryph stabbed a finger at Aneesa and tried to clarify her explanation. Jake raised his eyebrows, looking as if he was about to say, "Yeah, right." Then the parade absorbed a curious child right next to them, followed by the child's frantic mother. Jake's mouth dropped open, and his Adam's apple bobbed as he swallowed hard. He was about to speak when Gryph slapped her hand over her mouth, smothering a howl. Jake whirled about.

As each rank drew level with the entrance to the Civic Square, they disappeared. Two by two, the marchers vanished. Right before their eyes, people were disappearing into thin air.

Gryph clutched Jake's arm. "What now?"

"We follow," he said slowly. "We don't touch any of them, but we must follow."

"Are you crazy?" breathed Gryph.

"No. There's no rally scheduled. This isn't right. By the time the authorities realize what's going on, they'll all be gone. Some sort of fissure in time and space must have opened, and we have to follow while this is still happening." He shrugged. "Unless you'd rather just stand around and watch your best friend vanish?"

First Reading

What is Jake's explanation for why the procession is happening?

Close Reading

How would you summarize the odd events of Gryph's day?

Follow

Gryph waited until Aneesa's rank led the procession, hoping against hope that somehow they'd just stop, but they didn't. Aneesa and the chef vanished like the others.

"That settles it," muttered Gryph, and they dropped into formation behind the last pair. She couldn't believe she was following. She wanted to run away but didn't dare. A step before the vanishing point, Jake gave her a shaky thumbs up.

Gryph grabbed his arm, and with a single step, the world changed.

What had been a warm, northerly wind now bit with ice-sharpened teeth. High Street, Civic Square, and the bustle of downtown had been replaced by a hedge-lined country lane outside a ramshackle farmhouse. Gryph shivered as she watched the line of silent people, now packed single-file along the farm driveway—and all pointing at something out of sight behind the farmhouse.

"Too weird," said Jake. "They're no longer marching. The fissure must have closed. What are they all pointing at?"

Gryph couldn't spot Aneesa or the chef. She just hoped they were further down the line somewhere. "What do we do?"

WITH A SINGLE STEP, THE WORLD CHANGED

First Reading

Where do Gryph and Jake go after they step through the vanishing point?

"We try to find out what's happening here," said Jake grimly. He swung open the gate.

"This must be somebody's house. Apart from anything else, it's private property."

"Yes, so we knock at the door and ask permission. Maybe the people who live here have some idea of what's going on."

Jake's sharp rap on the door was answered by a gnarled old man wearing a bulky basketball jersey, wool trousers, and a faded winter cap.

"You've come about the dig?" The old man dragged on a pair of rubber boots, frowning at Gryph's shoes. "This way. Not that you're dressed for it, but your work's in the Incident Room. That's what you're here for, isn't it?" he added, suddenly doubtful.

"Pretty much," said Jake, nodding at Gryph. "I'm Jake, and this is my sister Gryph."

"Frank. In the old days it would have been Mr. Peden to you, but now Frank will do. Come along then. After you."

First Reading
Who is Frank?

Gryph sidled down the driveway, keeping Jake between her and the silent observers. She felt their eyes tracking her like target-finders. As if unaware of their audience, Frank shambled alongside.

Before Gryph could warn him, he brushed up against two of the spectators. He shuddered as he passed straight through them, muttering, "Bitter, that north wind. Hope you're not expecting a reception party. The archaeologists left yesterday without so much as a please or thank you." He chuckled. "My grandmother would have sworn the curse had got them."

7

"Curse?" Gryph asked.

Frank turned to look at Gryph with some interest. "So you can speak, can you?" he said. "Thought the Curse of the Silent might have got you. That curse would strike you dumb for life."

Around them, the mute audience nodded in unison. Gryph shot a look at Jake. His waxen pallor suggested he'd seen it, too.

As they rounded the corner of the house, the Silent vanished, then reformed in a semi-circle around a rectangular trench in the adjacent field.

"That's the dig," said Frank, pointing to it. "It's a useless bit of soil. Nothing ever grew there. Don't enter the trench until the pompous professor returns. The travel trailer is your Incident Room. The key's in the door. Power's on." He gave a crooked smile.

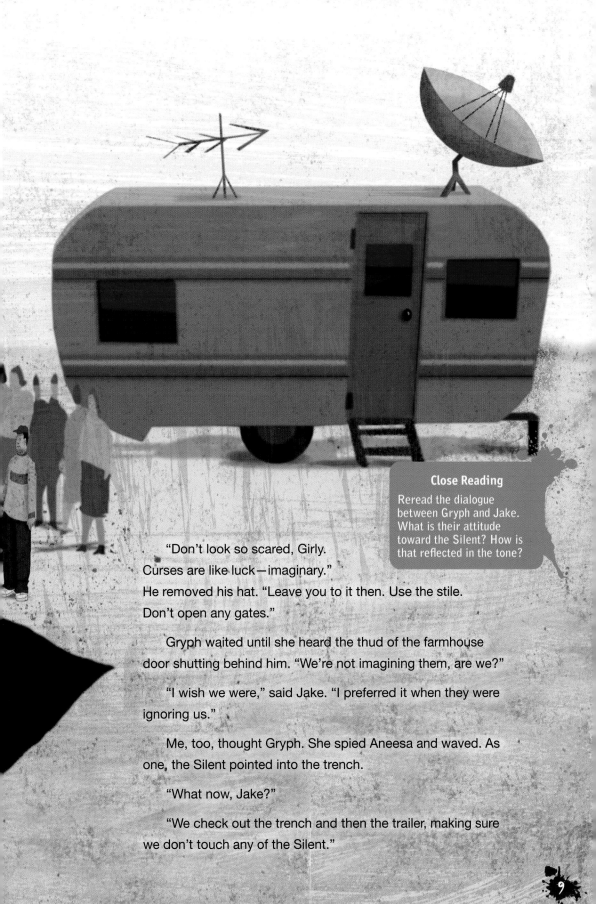

Close Reading

Reread the dialogue between Gryph and Jake. What is their attitude toward the Silent? How is that reflected in the tone?

"Don't look so scared, Girly. Curses are like luck—imaginary." He removed his hat. "Leave you to it then. Use the stile. Don't open any gates."

Gryph waited until she heard the thud of the farmhouse door shutting behind him. "We're not imagining them, are we?"

"I wish we were," said Jake. "I preferred it when they were ignoring us."

Me, too, thought Gryph. She spied Aneesa and waved. As one, the Silent pointed into the trench.

"What now, Jake?"

"We check out the trench and then the trailer, making sure we don't touch any of the Silent."

The Dig

The Silent fell back two paces, allowing the siblings a clear view of the gravelly trench. It was three feet deep and six feet long. A partially-uncovered stone protruded from the cutting at the base of the trench. As Jake craned his neck to look, the Silent mimicked his action.

Gryph rubbed her cold arms. No matter what Jake thought, following hadn't helped. They were stuck in this gray, desolate nowhere, freezing cold, with no clue what to do.

"The stone is carved," said Jake. "Not sure if it's writing . . . Gryph! Staring off into space isn't going to help."

"Where are we?"

"I have no idea," said Jake, crouching down beside the trench. Still as one, the Silent imitated him. "Northern Hemisphere somewhere, I'd guess."

"What?" asked Gryph. "Why is that?"

"The wind's a cold northerly. Down in Australia, our northerly winds come off the equator, so they would be warm, not cold. You see?"

"Jake—"

"Either say something useful or shut up," snapped Jake.

First Reading

Why does Jake believe they are in the Northern Hemisphere?

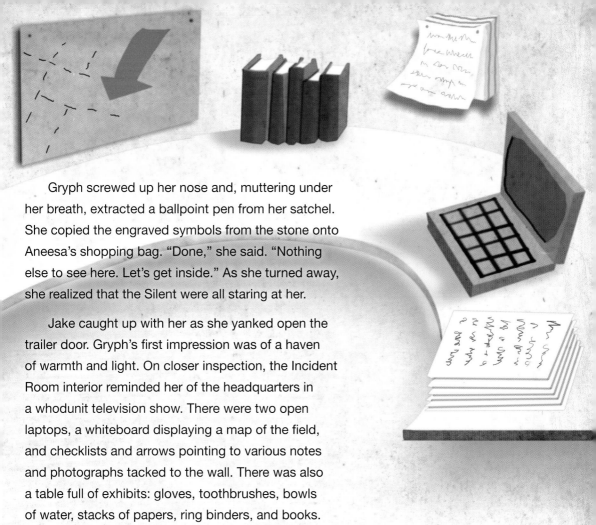

Gryph screwed up her nose and, muttering under her breath, extracted a ballpoint pen from her satchel. She copied the engraved symbols from the stone onto Aneesa's shopping bag. "Done," she said. "Nothing else to see here. Let's get inside." As she turned away, she realized that the Silent were all staring at her.

Jake caught up with her as she yanked open the trailer door. Gryph's first impression was of a haven of warmth and light. On closer inspection, the Incident Room interior reminded her of the headquarters in a whodunit television show. There were two open laptops, a whiteboard displaying a map of the field, and checklists and arrows pointing to various notes and photographs tacked to the wall. There was also a table full of exhibits: gloves, toothbrushes, bowls of water, stacks of papers, ring binders, and books. Among the notices on the whiteboard was one addressed to "Student Volunteers."

THE SILENT WERE ALL STARING AT HER

The checklist below instructed them to log the exhibits in the database: "Ensure that data entered is complete, and when handling artifacts, wear gloves at all times."

"Cool," said Jake. When Gryph didn't reply, he added, "Sorry for snapping before. I promised Mom I'd get you and Aneesa home safely. You're my responsibility."

First Reading
What do Gryph and Jake find in the Incident Room?

Except it was me who pushed Aneesa into it, thought Gryph. Her sleeve tickled the keyboard of the nearest laptop. "Hey, this is on."

"This one, too," said Jake. "Aha! The database."

He pulled up a chair and began tapping away as Gryph scrutinized the wall displays. A rubbing of an inscription caught her eye. She checked it against the copy she'd taken at the trench. They matched, as did the script on the left portion of a photocopy of an archaic painting. Beneath it were two sections of text. The intelligible one read:

Against malice, against mindlessness,
And against the untrue tongue,
Silence be my shield, silence be my armor,
And this stone my sharpest sword.
Strike mute those who oppose me,
And place locks forever on their tongues.

STRIKE MUTE THOSE WHO OPPOSE ME

"It is a curse," said Gryph.

"Not according to the professor," answered Jake. "This is his computer, and according to him, the engraving is nothing more than a warning. I'm with Frank and the professor. Check this out."

Gryph read the screen over his shoulder. "Hang on," she said. "The reference on the wall says that the stone will strike people dumb forever, and presumably the curse is passed on by touch. Don't you see that that's exactly what has happened?"

"We don't know that . . . ."

"We saw it. Both of us," insisted Gryph. As Jake shrugged, Gryph peeled a group photo off the wall and handed it to him. "I'll bet these are the archaeologists Frank mentioned. If you're so sure I'm wrong, go and check if they're among the Silent. If they are, then it's the curse."

First Reading
What test does Gryph propose to figure out if the engraving is a curse or just a warning?

The Curse Stone

After Jake left, Gryph settled down at the other computer—it seemed to belong to the professor's assistant—and executed a search for any files or folders with the word "curse" in the title. Within seconds, it returned a folder entitled "Curse History." Gryph clicked on it and scanned the file titles. Unsure where to start, she picked a word document.

The only intelligible words were "his," "man," "is," and "on." The other letters were run together in weird combinations of vowels and consonants. Gryph guessed that the recognizable words were unlikely to mean anything familiar.

Her third random selection turned up a document in English! It was about a despotic, local feudal lord who had invoked the Curse of the Silent in response to his tenants' refusal to pay their tithes. Gryph skipped over paragraphs about harvests, tithe calculation, estate boundaries, and census data. Nothing of interest sprang out at her, so she tried a search within the document. The word "curse" appeared just that once.

First Reading
Why does the feudal lord invoke the curse?

THE LORD THEN
SET ABOUT SILENCING
HIS OPPOSITION

The next file she opened was bilingual. There were more than a hundred pages, each split into two columns. Rather than skim-read them all, Gryph repeated her search for "curse" and moved from one instance to the next. At last she found what she was looking for—a subsection on "The Curse Stone."

It revealed that the lord had commissioned the carving of the curse stone in frustration over an extended tithe strike. His initial punishment of the strike leaders had had limited deterrent value. The tenants had responded by using coded rhymes as rallying calls. The lord then set about silencing his opposition.

Close Reading
In your own words, explain the "Curse of the Silent."

Gryph's cell phone beeped, and she flipped it open. It had connected to the local network, and fifteen texts had arrived. Four were answering her call for help, two were about school, three demanded to know what she was up to, and the remaining six were astonished at how many people had been reported missing that day. Gryph clapped her hands. The authorities were looking for them!

She was about to answer her texts when it occurred to her that no one was likely to look here. There was no reason to look overseas at all, let alone in the Northern Hemisphere. She'd seen no sign of helicopters or police—or for that matter, of anyone other than Frank. In spite of the texts, she and Jake were it as far as rescuers were concerned. Gryph's first priority had to be Aneesa and the curse. With a sigh, she put away her cell phone.

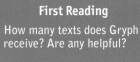

First Reading
How many texts does Gryph receive? Are any helpful?

THE ARCHAEOLOGISTS HAD PARTIALLY UNCOVERED THE CURSE STONE

She paged down and kept reading. In the last paragraph of the section, it said that an indeterminate number of years later, the silence was broken, and the curse stone was buried. Two adjacent maps illustrated the stone's burial place: one archaic and one modern. The modern map had the outline of a trench superimposed over it. There was no doubt about it. The archaeologists had partially uncovered the curse stone.

Gryph was dashing out to tell Jake when she froze in the trailer doorway. The Silent were surrounding the Incident Room. Worse still, Jake now stood, android-like, among them.

Close Reading
Notice in paragraph 2 that the author contrasts something happy with something tragic. What two events are being contrasted? What effect does this have on the emotion of the story?

17

Just Me

Gryph stepped back and slammed the door shut. She gulped, then lifted the corner of a curtain to verify that she was not mistaken. She wasn't. The Incident Room was surrounded, and she was trapped. Even if her shouts were audible, Frank couldn't help. Frank had first encountered the Silent after the fissure had closed. He would pass straight through them without seeing them. She couldn't.

"Just me," muttered Gryph. "Just me." She fumbled in her satchel for her cell phone. As her fingers closed around it, she hesitated. Who would she call? Who else could help? Another thought struck her then. What if the Silent were trying to help? What if their actions were clues? Gryph sat down and waved her hand in front of her face, trying to fan away the tears. She had to remain calm. She had to think.

THE INCIDENT ROOM WAS SURROUNDED SHE WAS TRAPPED

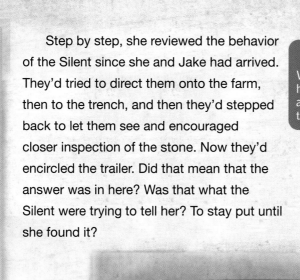

Step by step, she reviewed the behavior of the Silent since she and Jake had arrived. They'd tried to direct them onto the farm, then to the trench, and then they'd stepped back to let them see and encouraged closer inspection of the stone. Now they'd encircled the trailer. Did that mean that the answer was in here? Was that what the Silent were trying to tell her? To stay put until she found it?

First Reading

What theory does Gryph have for the Silent not allowing her to leave the trailer?

What could be the answer to a curse? Could there be some sort of antidote? Gryph opened a browser on the assistant's laptop and executed an Internet search. For an hour she tried various search strings across a number of search engines. Nothing in the screeds of results appeared useful.

Each time Gryph lifted the curtain to look out, a different pair of blank, android eyes stared back at her.

"Plan B," muttered Gryph. "I need a Plan B—a different approach." She reread the curse carefully, wondering if it held any clues. Nothing was obvious. Obvious, thought Gryph. Her mother always said, "Start with the obvious."

OK, Gryph thought, what was obvious? The title of the curse was the Curse of the Silent, and the opposite of silence—the antidote, in a way—was sound. Music perhaps? The last paragraph she'd read on the laptop hadn't mentioned anything about the curse being broken. It had been about the silence being broken. Gryph had no idea if she was on the right track, but at least it was a Plan B.

She set up a search of the assistant's hard drive, looking for files or folders with the word "music" in the title. While it searched, Gryph got up and leafed through the piles of paperwork. She had a vague recollection of seeing the corner of a handwritten document that may have been sheet music.

Halfway down the stack she found it, but it wasn't music.

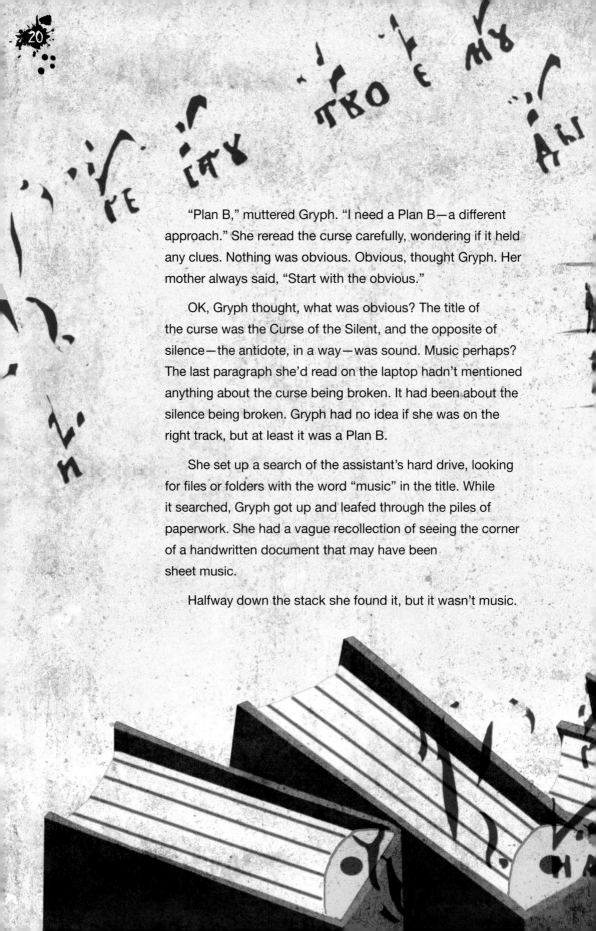

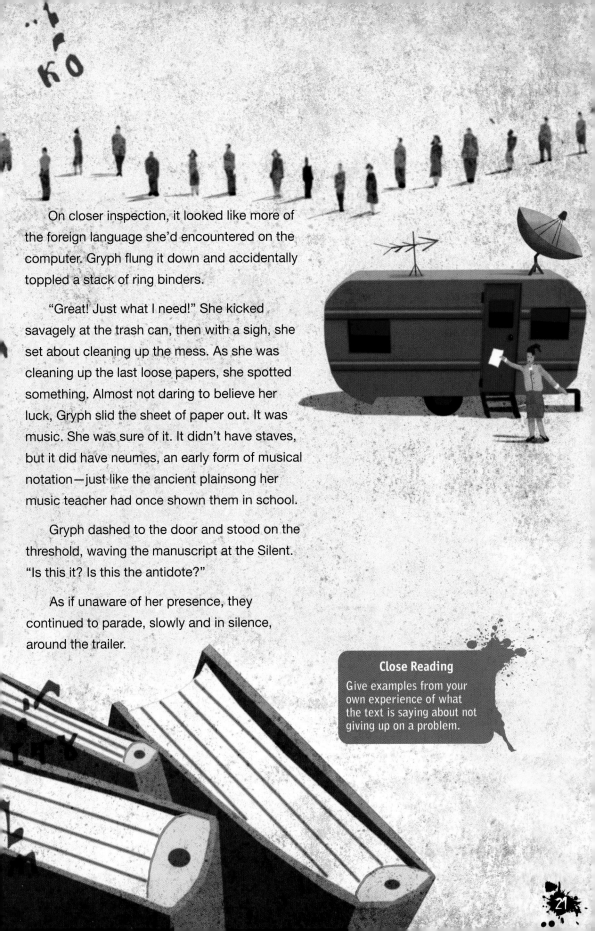

On closer inspection, it looked like more of the foreign language she'd encountered on the computer. Gryph flung it down and accidentally toppled a stack of ring binders.

"Great! Just what I need!" She kicked savagely at the trash can, then with a sigh, she set about cleaning up the mess. As she was cleaning up the last loose papers, she spotted something. Almost not daring to believe her luck, Gryph slid the sheet of paper out. It was music. She was sure of it. It didn't have staves, but it did have neumes, an early form of musical notation—just like the ancient plainsong her music teacher had once shown them in school.

Gryph dashed to the door and stood on the threshold, waving the manuscript at the Silent. "Is this it? Is this the antidote?"

As if unaware of her presence, they continued to parade, slowly and in silence, around the trailer.

Close Reading

Give examples from your own experience of what the text is saying about not giving up on a problem.

21

Breaking
the Silence

Gryph slumped back into the assistant's chair. As she dropped the sheet of music onto the keyboard, the screen flicked out of power-save mode. Her search had been successful. Better still, within the Curse History folder, it had found a file called "neume_music.doc."

"Yes!" breathed Gryph. Sure enough, the document contained an image identical to the sheet Gryph had found. It was identified as the "Melody of Healing." The introduction noted that the music was to be played over the exposed curse stone to heal it. The word "heal" was highlighted.

"The stone will heal, but what about the Silent?" murmured Gryph. As she moved the mouse over the highlighted word, a note popped open explaining that both the stone and its victims were healed by the music. It would break the silence afflicting the victims and temporarily expunge the curse from the stone's surface. Once the carving was removed, the stone could be safely buried. In bold, someone had added, "Don't delete. Just in case."

GRYPH TOOK A DEEP BREATH AND, WITH HER PHONE IN HER HAND, OPENED THE TRAILER DOOR

Gryph sat up. This time she had the answer. She knew what she needed to do, but how? She couldn't read the music, so singing it wasn't an option. Then it occurred to her that, if the professor's assistant had thought they might possibly need it, surely there would be a sound file somewhere on the computer. A search for mp3 files revealed neume.mp3.

"Gotcha!" yelled Gryph as she connected to the Internet and began uploading the mp3 file to her personal Web site. Then, crossing her fingers, she downloaded it from the site onto her cell phone.

She took a deep breath and, with her phone in her hand, opened the trailer door. The Silent were still circling.

She pressed play. For a split second, nothing happened. Then, as the slow, melancholy melody began to sound, the Silent vanished. As before, they reformed around the trench.

First Reading

How does Gryph get the mp3 file onto her cell phone?

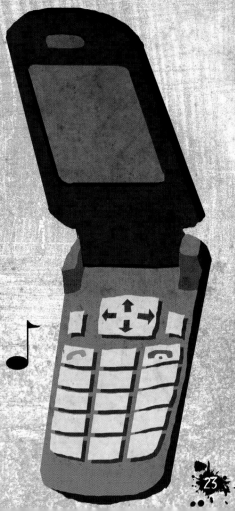

Close Reading

Does the author's inclusion of technology help or hinder the credibility of the story? Why or why not?

Buoyed by her success, Gryph followed. Again, the Silent fell back, allowing her access. Gryph shot a look over her shoulder at the farmhouse, then she clambered down into the trench.

Half a step away from the stone, she again pressed play. With each note that sounded, a symbol smudged into obscurity on the stone's surface. Gryph held her breath as the final line began to fade away. She was unsure how many notes were needed to cleanse the last few buried words.

As the concluding note died away, an exultant cheer erupted. Mid-syllable, the world changed once more.

GRYPH HELD HER BREATH AS THE FINAL LINE BEGAN TO FADE AWAY

First Reading

What happens each time Gryph presses play on her phone?

Gryph and Aneesa were standing wide-eyed
amid the bustle of downtown. The warm, northerly
wind of home swirled about them, lifting the chill
from their bones. Her shopping bag back in her
hand, Aneesa looked around her, as if unable to
believe her eyes.

"Can you talk? Are you all right?" asked Gryph.

"Yes . . . "

Gryph flung her arms around Aneesa's neck.
"Thank goodness. What a relief!"

"So I wasn't imagining it then? It happened?" whispered Aneesa.

Gryph nodded. "I'm so sorry. I promise I'll never do that again. I'll never push you into anything I'm not prepared to do myself."

"You going to promise me, too?" asked Jake, bounding up beside them.

"What?" Aneesa and Gryph asked together.

"You pushed me into it, too. Remember?"

"No," said Gryph. "I just told you to go out and look. I didn't make you touch them."

"Whatever," said Jake. "You fixed it, that's the main thing. Not bad for my little sister, I suppose."

"What about the others?" asked Aneesa.

Jake shrugged. "Probably back to square one like us. I just hope you're not planning on bragging too much about your heroics, Gryph," he said, softening it with a big grin.

First Reading
Why does Gryph think the professor's assistant is the real hero?

Gryph shook her head. If anyone was a hero, it was the professor's assistant. It was the assistant's research that had led to the solution, and Gryph hoped that the professor had learned from what had happened. The archaeologists had to rebury the stone while they had the opportunity— the consequences of not doing so weren't worth thinking about.

She linked her arm through Aneesa's. "Let's get out of here. I don't know about you two, but I've had enough of weird marchers for one day."

Close Reading
How would you summarize the main plot points of the story?

Think About the Text

MAKING CONNECTIONS

Which of the following connections can you make to the characters, plot, setting, and themes of *The Silent*?

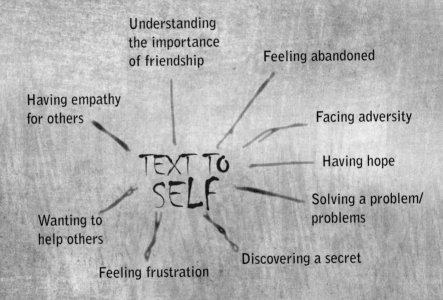

Understanding the importance of friendship

Feeling abandoned

Having empathy for others

Facing adversity

Having hope

TEXT TO SELF

Solving a problem/problems

Wanting to help others

Discovering a secret

Feeling frustration

TEXT TO TEXT/MEDIA

Talk about texts/media you have read, listened to, or seen that have similar themes. Compare the treatment of theme and the differing author styles.

TEXT TO WORLD

Talk about situations in the world that connect to elements in the story.

Planning a Fantasy Story

1 Think about what defines fantasy

Fantasy stories feature imaginary worlds and magical or supernatural events. The reader is called upon to believe and accept an alternative version of reality.

2 Think about the plot

Fantasy stories include action that depends on real-world problems or conflict that are solved in a fantastical or magical way.

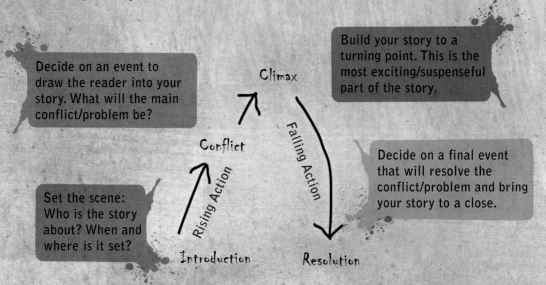

Decide on an event to draw the reader into your story. What will the main conflict/problem be?

Build your story to a turning point. This is the most exciting/suspenseful part of the story.

Decide on a final event that will resolve the conflict/problem and bring your story to a close.

Set the scene: Who is the story about? When and where is it set?

Climax

Conflict

Rising Action

Falling Action

Introduction

Resolution

3 Think about the characters

Explore:

- how they perceive their world
- how they respond to these fantastic places, events, and time periods
- how they think, feel, and act—and what motivates their behavior

- the social structures of the imaginary community and how they affect the characters' status, appearance, and behavior

4 Decide on the setting

atmosphere/ mood location → time

Remember: Setting is an important part of creating a successful fantasy story. The identifying traits of fantasy are the inclusion of fantastic elements that may be hidden in or leak into an apparently real-world setting. The fantastical world should expand the reader's horizon and should be developed in detail to support the story line.

Writing a Fantasy Story

HAVE YOU . . .

- dealt with real-world problems and solved them in a fantastical/magical way?

- used limited explanations for strange behaviors/events/objects?

- provided a window into another reality and possibility?

- explored social laws, values, and beliefs of a different/extraordinary time and place?

- developed events that could be credible?

- used the setting to transport the reader to an imaginary world?

- used elements of science/physics principles to "dress up" the fantasy content?

- included elements/characters with special powers?

- created a consistent/logical story despite elements of magic and the supernatural?

DON'T FORGET TO REVISIT YOUR WRITING.

DO YOU NEED TO CHANGE, ADD, OR DELETE ANYTHING TO IMPROVE YOUR STORY?